SPEECH

OF THE

HON. WILLIAM B. REED,

ON

THE PRESIDENTIAL QUESTION.

DELIVERED BEFORE THE

NATIONAL DEMOCRATIC ASSOCIATION.

Philadelphia, September 4, 1860.

THE PRESIDENTIAL QUESTION.

FELLOW-CITIZENS:—

I learn that one of the newspapers which favours the election of Mr. Lincoln, has lately uttered a sort of challenge, or taunt, or conjecture, as to the silence, thus far, of those whom it calls the "Breckinridge leaders" in this city, and that I am, by name, appealed to as one of them. While I disclaim any such distinction, I have no disposition to conceal my opinions; and have come here to-night so far to repel the taunt as to try to show in a few precise, and, I hope, inoffensive words, why I think, and wish others to think, especially the citizens of Pennsylvania and Philadelphia, that it will conduce to our social and political well-being, and to our material interests—to which none are insensible—that Mr. Breckinridge should be elected President. I do not come to counsel, for I have no right to do so; but I have some practical suggestions to make, which, I trust, may be listened to.

In a political atmosphere, heated as ours is, it is difficult to speak without offence; but I shall endeavour to do so. The danger just now don't seem to be of talking unkindly of our legitimate adversaries. It is in another direction; and in that direction, if possible, I do not mean to be led or driven. I have no words of offence to utter, and I regret that others have, as to Judge Douglas. My personal relations to him and his, though very slight, have always been friendly and respectful. I was absent from the country, too far away to be reached by the asperities of our politics when those difficulties occurred which seem to have alienated Mr. Douglas from the Democratic party. I listened to his last and most elaborate speech in the Senate in vindication of his opinions, if without conviction, certainly with interest. But here in candour I am obliged to stop; for when I see the course of his organ here, and of many of his friends,—when I read their bitter vituperation (for the word is not too strong) of all who differ from them,—when I see that they have imported speakers as if for the special purpose of defaming Pennsylvania men,—when the President, in one speech, is likened to Tiberius, and his approaching retirement compared with the infamies of Capreæ; and in another (I refer to a revised report of Mr. Foote's late speech at Harrisburg), the Attorney-General of the United States, a man against whose private and public character no whisper of reproach was ever uttered, is denounced by name,—when such men, our own fellow-citizens, are thus, in violation of common decency, defamed by Judge Douglas's leading friends, I beg to be excused from the association, or for thinking any political end of value enough to be gained or sought by such means.

Our other friends or adversaries—for I really hardly know which to call them—across the street, the Bell and Everett men, are entitled to great consideration. Theirs is the unquestioned merit that they claim to be, in organization, in aim, and in policy, national. No more national men live than Mr. Ingersoll, who is a recognized leader here, and Judge King, and Mr. Fuller. I have been too long a reader of Whig newspapers not to do justice to John Bell. Mr. Everett's record is that of a thoroughly national man. Years ago, in 1826, he said in a speech in Congress, that in the event of a servile insurrection, though no soldier, he would shoulder his musket and fight for the rights of the South; and for this sentiment he has been the mark of Abolition ribaldry ever since. Mr. Crittenden voted in the Senate for Mr. Davis's resolutions on the territorial question, which is the Breckinridge platform. Towards these gentlemen, and their principles, so far as they have been made known, we all have a respectful feeling, which

I should be sorry to have checked by foolish letters or foolish speeches, imputing sectionalism to Mr. Breckinridge. They know better. Such defamation is not worthy the lips of gentlemen and men of sense.

We have no bids to make to the Bell and Everett party. We don't insult them by threats. Had it not been for the division that has been created in the Democratic ranks, we might have seen, before this, a great conservative combination, which would have wrested even New England from its thraldom, and struck Abolition a triumphant blow, even in its heart of Massachusetts. The "solid men of Boston," to whom Mr. Seward made his recent appeal, are national men. They were Mr. Webster's friends when Mr. Seward opposed him. They are Mr. Everett's friends now, when Mr. Seward comes, and almost within earshot of Mr. Everett's house, defies him. I believe the national sentiment of the country will yet awaken to the necessity of combined and effective action. How, or by what means, I do not pretend to say. It may be at the last moment,—it may be on the very edge of the final contest. No one ought to say a word to render it impossible. No one ought to be restless and fidgety in promoting it. If it does happen, depend on it, a great element of its successful action will be the organized Democracy of Pennsylvania,—the friends in every county of Breckinridge and Lane. Its integrity must be respected. It will be time enough when, by the spontaneous co-operation of patriotic men throughout the commonwealth, Mr. Foster shall be elected Governor, as he easily can be.

So much for side issues, which I am sorry to have to talk about, but which it would be mere affectation to ignore. Now, for the common enemy. Of Mr. Lincoln, whose election I consider full of threatened evil to the Union and to Pennsylvania, I have no reason to speak, but with due personal consideration. It is very much in his favour that he was nominated at Chicago and is now recommended to the people, as a concession to the moderation of the country, and that his nomination was effected by the revolt of Pennsylvania against the dictation of New York. The New York politicians pooh-poohed Pennsylvania candidates, and Pennsylvania plucked up spirit enough to punish New York by nominating Mr. Lincoln, and then New York returned the compliment, by giving us a free-trade, free-soil Vice-President in Mr. Hamlin. Whether Pennsylvania will be further punished in the long run, for her independence, I do not pretend to say. Time, in fact, can only determine, whether, for what she dared to do, Pennsylvania is to be so rewarded or so insulted, but I confess I like Mr. Lincoln all the better, because at this risk, he was the nominee of Pennsylvania. I am quite aware that another solution has been given to this result, and that high authority may be cited to show that Mr. Seward was defeated for other reasons than his unpopularity in Pennsylvania. In the "New York Evening Post" of May 23, edited by Mr. Bryant, now a Republican elector, I find this passage:—

"But there was another cause of Mr. Seward's failure, which does not appear from any part of the proceedings of the Convention, and which yet was more potent than any other. It deserves to be plainly stated for the instruction of men in public life. Mr. Seward lost the nomination through the misconduct of some of his warmest and oldest friends. Our readers are not now to hear for the first time of the shamelessly corrupt conduct of the New York Legislature, both during the past winter and the winter previous, with a Republican majority in both branches. Nothing could have happened more injurious to the prospects of Mr. Seward than the almost open venality on one side and no less shameless subornation of venality on the other among many of those who claimed to be the most zealous political friends of Mr. Seward. Thousands of men who were friendly to Mr. Seward's nomination a year since were thrown into the utmost consternation by these enormities, and asked whether, in case of Mr. Seward's election to the Presidency, all this corruption was to be transferred to Washington. His personal integrity they did not allow themselves to question, but they felt the strongest distrust, to use the mildest term, of those who were to go into office with him. To the strength of this feeling, and to its contagion, spreading beyond the State, Mr. Seward's failure is owing. Had our legislature but conducted itself with ordinary propriety during the two last winters, he would have been at this moment the Republican candidate for the Presidency."

All this may be so, but I am content with the other reason. Either is quite enough.

But grave objections to Mr. Lincoln have been revealed since his nomination, to which, without personal disparagement, I beg leave to call your attention. Since the Convention at Chicago, Mr. Lincoln, with one exception, has maintained a resolute and prudent silence. The discussion with Judge Douglas in their canvass was characterized on his part by frankness and ability, and in the presence of a wary antagonist ready to take advantage of any indiscretion, by moderation. Little more than a year ago he wrote a letter, in which he was betrayed into language, which, though not very precise, and a little ambitious, was ominous. It was this: "This is a world of compensations, and he who would be no slave, must consent to have no slave. Those who deny freedom to others, deserve it not for themselves, and under a just God, cannot long retain it." It is not easy to say what this means, but it has an ugly look. Since his nomination, Mr. Lincoln has spoken once, and once too often. I refer to his speech at Springfield, about four weeks ago, which was the more significant, as he appears to have been taken by surprise, and to have spoken out, under an impulse, his inner thoughts. There is, I believe, a religious sect, called "Progressive Friends,"—so, in politics, there are *progressive* Republicans, and to this class it would seem Mr. Lincoln belongs. I infer this from his speech, which either means this, or means nothing. His language was: "My friends, you will fight for this cause, four years hence, as you now fight for it, *and even stronger than you now fight for it*, though I may be dead and gone." Now, in all candour, I ask, what does this mean?—what does Mr. Lincoln mean by an adjourned or continued conflict, by his "stronger fight" hereafter. Does it mean there is to be no repose, no settlement, no finality, under his administration? The "fight" is to go on—nay, it is to be "stronger" then than now. Not content with the victory of a compact North, over the stricken and insulted South, the arms are not to be laid aside,—the array is not to be broken,—the entrenched camp is not to be dismantled,—peace and conciliation are not even hinted at. Domestic slavery, driven by a triumphant executive and congressional majority, from the territories, is to be beleaguered in the States. It is to exist by sufferance,—it is to be destroyed by compression, and the varnished, plausible, and deceptive Republicanism of 1860 is to become the aggressive Abolitionism of 1864. So says Mr. Lincoln, if his language has any meaning, or be anything but the clumsiest rhetoric.

Such was the utterance—no doubt the unguarded and genuine utterance, in the West, at Springfield, Mr. Lincoln's home, on the 9th of last month, August. This was, if I mistake not, on the Thursday of one week, on which day, or thereabouts, Mr. Seward sets out to look after Judge Douglas, in New England, and arrived in Boston, on Monday the 13th, and then and there, as I have said, close to Edward Everett's home, as if in insult and defiance, he reproduces his doctrine of "irrepressible conflict," *ipsissimis verbis*, and adds with emphasis—speaking I fear by authority—(I quote his very words), "Abraham Lincoln confesses his obligation to the higher law, which the Sage of Quincy proclaimed, and avows himself for weal or for woe, life or death, a soldier on the side of freedom, in the irrepressible conflict between freedom and slavery." This is plain language. This is not careless or clumsy rhetoric, to which Mr. Seward is not addicted. He always carefully elaborates.

Thus speaks Mr. Lincoln for himself at one end of the line, and thus speaks Mr. Seward for him at the other; and I beg you to observe, so startling was this development of the animating spirit, the true design of the Republican party, that the leading organs of Mr. Lincoln in this city, who are busily engaged in seducing "the solid men" of Philadelphia into the belief that he and his party are not agitators of this slavery question, have never ventured to publish Mr. Seward's recent speeches. Not that they are very punctilious either; for, about the time when Mr. Lincoln was making what looked very much like an Abolition speech in Illinois, and Mr. Seward two or three in New England, there appeared in the ablest and least radical of the Republican newspapers of this city, a translation, in the form of an editorial article, of Victor Hugo's pamphlet on Italy, in which John Brown is canonized by name, as a proto-martyr, the action of the law in Virginia is denounced as "infamous," America is stigmatized as "leaning to darkness," and "the negro is bid to hope." I am quite aware that the editor, who tries his best to be a conservative man, was absent when the railing of this crazy Frenchman was reproduced—but it did appear; was read by thousands; was added to the stock of wretched literature which has anti-slavery for its basis, and gladdened the hearts of those who, with Mr. Lincoln and Mr. Seward and Mr. Sumner, look forward to the good time of the "irrepressible conflict," "the stronger fight," when, to use Mr. Seward's words in another connection, "the banner will be unfurled with safety in the slave States." Lord Brougham and Victor Hugo, an English and a French Abolitionist, insult us at the same time. The New York Tribune thinks Lord Brougham did what was right, and the Lincoln papers of Philadelphia reproduce the ravings of the French enthusiast, with the faintest possible expression of dissent.

When in 1855, Mr. Sumner made his anti-slavery harangue in the Senate, the public mind revolted at it, and nothing but the act of violence which it provoked saved it from universal condemnation. Now, in 1860, he makes a much worse speech, more defamatory, more acrimonious, more grotesquely malignant, and Republican senators listen with contentment, and Mr. Sumner has an ovation in the city of New York, where, amidst bright eyes, dimmed only by tears of sympathy, and tumultuous cheers, he makes a speech for the Republican candidate, worse than any he ever uttered; and Wendell Phillips preaches aggressive abolition in Philadelphia, and Mr. Curtis, a leading delegate at Chicago, has to be protected by the strong hand of the law, as he invokes sympathy for those who would have been glad to make a new Cawnpore on the banks of the Potomac. Mr. Sumner's last triumph is the nomination of a "Radical Republican" as Governor of Massachusetts.

Nay, further, I hold in my hand a book published in New York, and called the "Republican Campaign Hand-Book," an authoritative exposition of doctrines, north of a certain parallel, and I find its moral to be in so many words, that Lincoln's election is but a step in the march of "progressive humanity," leading to the grand triumph of emancipation everywhere. Its language is:—

"The people of those States where liberty is not stifled by cowardly and brutal force, have it in their power to insure political reform, and save the grand expanse of territory, of over one thousand million of acres in the West, from the wreck and shame of slavery. This they can do constitutionally, without infringing upon Southern privileges; and by so restricting the evil, and saving further land from its devastations, *they will lead the way to yet higher achievements*. Other nations beckon us on: England, her House of Lords roused by the memorable logic and eloquence of a Brougham, struck the chains off all her slaves, and each rising and setting sun does homage to the majesty of the achievement, over the hills and vales of her happy islands. Russia, with twenty million serfs, is, at the fiat of her best Emperor, about to touch them with the Ithuriel spear of emancipation, so that their moral nature may reach the skies. Shall we, then, with such glorious examples of the good, the generous, and the right, retroact, absolve ourselves from our gallant past, cut off our brilliant future, and be stifled in essential barbarism? In this epoch, when science flies on the wings of love, can we sanction the worship of hate and cruelty? This, and not less than this, is contained in the solution of the great questions before us. We have either to succumb to, *or to triumph over*, the slave power. There is no middle course. We must either have the black flag of slavery, or one scintillating with freedom, to symbolize our home and country. Our irreversible word, then, should be for Liberty—circling our lakes and seas; traversing our mountains and prairies; covering our cities and villages; going forth in many ships over many waters: liberty for the poor, the exiled, and the oppressed; liberty of sense and soul, of thought and speech, of aspiration and action."

And further still, a great element of the supposed Republican strength in the Northwestern States, is that of the German Abolitionists. They were a recognized power at Chicago. They are a recognized power in the canvass; and freed from the restraints which habits of early training and education impose, speak out boldly. Their leader is an individual named Carl Shurz (who was a delegate I believe at Chicago), and in his speech delivered a few days ago at St. Louis, and republished in the Republican journals with high praise, I find the following, which I quote without comment, begging the moderate Republicans of this vicinage to meditate on it, and see whither they are being led:—

"Look around you and see how lonesome you are in this wide world of ours. As far as modern civilization throws its rays, what people, what class of society, is there like you? Cry out into the world your wild and guilty fantasy of property in man, and every echo responds with a cry of horror or contempt; every breeze, from whatever point of the compass it may come, brings you a verdict of condemnation. There is no human heart that sympathizes with your cause, unless it sympathizes with the cause of despotism in every form. There is no human voice to cheer you on in your struggle; there is no human eye that has a tear for your reverses; no link of sympathy between the common cause of the great human brotherhood and you. You hear of emancipation in Russia, and wish it should fail. You hear of Italy rising, and fear the spirit of liberty should become contagious. Where all mankind rejoices you tremble. Where all mankind love you hate. Where all mankind curses you sympathize.

"And in this appalling solitude you stand alone against a powerful world, alone against a great century, fighting, hopeless as the struggle of the Indians, against the onward march of civilization. Use all the devices which the inventive genius of despotism may suggest, and yet how can you resist? In every little village school-house, the little children who learn to read and write are plotting against you; in every laboratory of science, in every machine-shop, the human mind is working the destruction of your idol. You cannot make an attempt to keep pace with the general progress of mankind without plotting against yourselves. Every steam-whistle, every puffing locomotive, is sounding the shriek of liberty into your ears. From the noblest instincts of our hearts down to the sordid greediness of gain, every impulse of human nature is engaged in this universal conspiracy. How can you resist? Where are your friends in the North? Your ever-ready supporters are scattered to the winds, as by enchantment, never to unite again. Hear them, trying to save their own fortunes, swear with treacherous eagerness that they have nothing in common with you, And your opponents? Your boasts have lost their charm, your threats have lost their terrors upon them. The attempt is idle to cloak the sores of Lazarus with the lion skin of Hercules. We know you. Every one of your boasts is understood as a disguised moan of weakness—every shout of defiance as a disguised cry for mercy. That game is played out. Do not deceive yourselves. This means not only the destruction of a party—this means the defeat of a cause. Be shrewder than the shrewdest, braver than the bravest—it is all in vain; your cause is doomed.

"And in the face of all this, you insist upon hugging, with dogged stubbornness, your fatal infatuation. *Why not, with manly boldness, swing round into the grand march of progressive humanity?* You say it cannot be done to-day. Can it be done to-morrow? Will it be easier twenty, fifty years hence, when the fearful increase of the negro population will have aggravated the evils of slavery an hundredfold, and with it the difficulties of extinction? Did you ever think of this? *The final crisis will come, with the inexorable certainty of fate, the more terrible the longer it is delayed.* Will you content yourselves with the criminal words, 'After me the deluge?' Is that the inheritance you mean to leave to coming generations? an inheritance of disgrace, crime, blood, destruction? Hear me, slaveholders of America! If you have no sense of right, no appreciation of your own interests, I entreat, I implore you, have at least pity for your children!

"I hear the silly objection, that your sense of honour forbids you to desert your cause: Sense of honour! Imagine a future generation standing round the tombstone of the bravest of you, and reading the inscription: 'Here lies a gallant man, who lived and died true to the cause—of human slavery.' What will the verdict be? His very progeny will disown him, and exclaim, 'He must have been either a knave or a fool!' *There is not one of you who, if he could rise from the dead a century hence, would not gladly exchange his epitaph for that of the meanest of those who were hung at Charlestown.*"

Surely, my fellow-citizens, in all this there is startling progress. When, in 1856, Mr. Seward made his Rochester speech, he soon felt he had gone too far at that date, and, if my memory does not deceive me, tried to explain it away. In his speech last winter in the Senate his offensive doctrines were clothed in the rhetorical dress of "capital" and "labour;" but now this thin disguise is thrown away. He revives his ancient "irrepressible" theory boldly and defiantly, as if he were proud of his phrases. He goes to Bangor, and in compliment to *his* Vice-President, talks to the Maine fishermen of their superiority to cotton-planters and sugar-growers, and their not being governed by the "slave-owner's lash,"—and thence to Boston, and, in the midst of its national men, the Everetts, and Winthrops, and Appletons, and Hillards, and Curtis's, and Lunts, insults the South by a new war-cry of defiance. There is, I say, progress in this; and Mr. Lincoln, with the certainty, as his friends claim, of triumph swelling in his heart, starts from his seclusion, and tells us that all this is nothing to what is to be by-and-by—"the prologue to the swelling act" of the great theme hereafter—as Wendell Phillips honestly said, "the entering wedge, to be driven home," the skirmish before the "stronger fight;" in short, but the beginning of the end of slavery as an institution anywhere.

It was in the same speech Mr. Seward intimated, that one of the great results of a Republican triumph would be that the President should send abroad, as the diplomatic representatives of the country, individuals who, unlike those who for many years have filled these posts, would concur in the general sentiment of reprobation of slavery all over the civilized world; in other words, those who would relish Lord Brougham's sneers, and Victor Hugo's insults, and take into close communion, on terms of social equality, any negro who might have the advantage of such sponsors. Now, with some opportunities of observation, I must be permitted to say that no such state of feeling or action exists as the Republican leader supposes. It seems to me that our representatives abroad, so far as I met them, found other things to do, or think, or talk about, than slavery, or anti-slavery. As a general rule, they are silent on the subject; and it will be an evil day when this silence is broken, and the traveller from South Carolina or Georgia finds his ambassador an Abolition propagandist. Such, we are told, they are to be. But, gentlemen, in this connection I have one other experience which was most painful. Coming from the extreme East, where it was my misfortune to find too few of my countrymen, and approaching those lines of travel where the rich and the idle, and the cultivated Americans are found in great numbers, I looked to meet that sympathy with the spirit of our institutions which nothing more intensifies than a long exile such as mine. Instead of which, the sentiment I encountered among my countrymen—many of the most intelligent and accomplished (generally, I admit, from one section of the United States)—was one I can only describe as disloyalty, the perverse sentimentalism which is the living spirit of this anti-slavery excitement—a sublimated sort of morality—an æsthetic communion with the unreal and morbid incongruity with the real. Americans, who should have loved their country, and revered its Constitution, and resented insults to its constituted authorities, I found hostile, and disloyal, and defamatory; and the one cry was, sympathy with virtue-proud England,—virtue-proud on this subject mainly, and antagonism to home, so long as slavery was a recognized institution among us. Of course there were exceptions—numerous exceptions—and among them I recall one, the most brilliant of American writers, from whose lips or whose pen no word of disloyalty, that I am aware of, ever fell,—who loves his country as it is, with or without slavery,—and who, unlike Abolition agitators, in his last wonderful work of genius, has spoken of his own dear native land as one where *"no gloomy wrong exists."* But most else was sad disloyalty and disaffection, to be increased a thousand-fold when Governor Seward's day of promise dawns, and we are to have abroad diplomatic detractors of our domestic institutions,—panegyrists of that great scheme of hypocritical philanthropy which emanates from Exeter Hall,—sympathizers of Lord Brougham and Victor Hugo.

I am not, I think, overstating this. I have no disposition to misconstrue either what Mr. Lincoln or Mr. Seward, or Mr. Sumner, or any one else has said, but I ask any candid friend of either, to take the aggregate speech-making of a fortnight ago at Boston and Springfield,—to take one as a gloss on the other,—Seward's Coke on Lincoln's Littleton,—and explain to me its other and truer meaning; and if there be one, or if, as sometimes happens, but not often, with an expert rhetorician like Mr. Seward, or a rough, plain-spoken man like Mr. Lincoln, there be no meaning at all in these phrases, I shall be most happy to admit I have done injustice.

The sad conviction presses on me, that the animating spirit of the Republican party, however individuals may honestly disclaim it, is anti-slavery fanaticism, enthusiastic sentimentalism, founded on the false ethical principle that slavery, as it exists in this country is wrong, *per se,* and that under the obligation of the higher law, to which Mr. Seward has pledged Mr. Lincoln, there can be no covenant or constitution, which binds us to protect it. Take away from the Republican organization the anti-slavery element, the sentiment which sways New England and the extreme Northwest, and it would be the merest shell that ever dignified itself with the name of party. Keep within it that spirit, active, energetic, honest, if you please; for, most fanaticism, from the days of John of Leyden, is honest, and you have it, as it is—a terrible, dangerous, aggressive antagonist, in whose grasp, such conventionalities as laws and constitutions, are crushed without a scruple.

I am quite aware that this progress—this increasing indifference to the obligation to conventional duty on this point—to which I have referred, is claimed to be a proof of the triumph of a great moral process or principle. I question much if the intelligence of our countrymen is yet sublimated to this point; mine certainly is not; I still revere the authority of those who have gone before me; I still swear by the Constitution, as it is judicially construed, and I dread that social and political revolution, now so imminent, which is to inaugurate the new school of political obedience to a higher law than the Constitution, to which Mr. Seward has pledged Mr. Lincoln and his administration.

I have said, gentlemen, that the aggressive spirit of Abolitionism, is not confined to New England and New York, but that it exists in its most acrid form, in the region where Mr. Lincoln lives, and which now, so unanimously sustains him. We are so much in the habit of worrying ourselves and occupying our minds with this vexed and prospective question of territorial sovereignty or subjection, that we forget other more dangerous anomalies—more pestilent difficulties. One occurs to me, which a recent outrage on the laws makes painfully impressive, though it, like the abolition burnings in Texas hardly yet suppressed, is lost sight of, so busy are we, with Douglas or Anti-Douglas, Lecompton or Anti-Lecompton. I refer to the resistance—the successful resistance—to the fugitive slave law in the Northwest.

This is not the place (though the topic is full of interest) to trace the course of lawlessness and defiance, which has characterized the conceded

Republican States, as to the law for the recapture of runaway negroes. The trouble began eighteen years ago, when a New England judge, by a dexterous device (for which his biographer claims credit) annulled all local auxiliary legislation on the subject. Before that, as I well remember, the recapture and surrender of fugitives as property was as simple and easy and tranquil a judicial act as the surrender of a fugitive from justice. The notion had not even germinated then that slaves could not be "property." They had been so considered from the beginning. As early as 1791, Washington described them in so many words as "property," and exerted his whole official influence for their recapture as such, and this before any fugitive slave act was passed. Still earlier, in 1786, Washington lent his personal aid to recover for a friend a runaway; and in a letter now in existence in this city, deplored the existence of combinations to defeat this very right of property which the sentimentalism of to-day considers such an abomination. "I have sent the negro boy," writes Washington to Mr. Drayton, "under the care of a trusty overseer, to be shipped to you (at Charleston). When he arrived at Baltimore it was necessary to commit him to jail for security. He has since escaped to Philadelphia." And then he adds: "The gentleman to whose care I sent him has promised every endeavour to apprehend him, but it is not easy to do this when there are numbers who would rather facilitate the escape of slaves than apprehend them when runaways." Washington, unlike Carl Shurz, did not think property in a slave "a wild and guilty phantasy." Since 1822 this notion of progressive humanity has grown till the wrong culminates in the Personal Liberty Bill of Massachusetts, an existing statute, of which every Republican approves, and in the successful defiance of the acts of Congress and the federal judiciary in Wisconsin, one of Mr. Lincoln's surest States. For this, I don't mean to say or intimate that Mr. Lincoln is responsible, but when I remember that, at the Chicago Convention, Judge McLean was almost contemptuously thrust aside, as he had been in 1856, because he had vigorously sustained the Fugitive Slave Act, and Mr. Bates, in spite of Mr. Greeley's indorsement, because he lived in a slave State; and Mr. Lincoln was nominated, as beyond these reproaches, we may be excused for fears and suspicions and distrust.

The Wisconsin case, to which I have referred, is familiar to every lawyer, but perhaps not so generally known as it ought to be, and illustrates the revolutionary character of northwestern abolitionism. Without going into detail, it may be thus stated: A fugitive slave, one whose relation had been proved, and who had been, under the law, ordered to be given up to his master, was rescued from the marshal by violence, and, I presume, fled to that region of safe refuge, Canada. The chief agent in this violence was tried in the District Court of the United States, before a jury, convicted and sentenced, just as three negroes were a few months ago in this city. No sooner was this done, than the Supreme Court of Wisconsin issued a *habeas corpus*, brought up the prisoner, and set him at liberty. Nay, further, the court ordered the clerk not to make a record or exemplification of the judgment, so as to defeat, as they thought, the revisory power of the Supreme Court of the United States. It was by mere accident that a record was obtained, and when the action of the State court was reversed at Washington, and the criminal put back in jail, we learn from the newspapers, that a mob lately rescued him and set him at liberty. He now defies the law. Now, my fellow-citizens, if this had been done in South Carolina, it would have been called Southern insolence and nullification, and perhaps treason, and yet, when it is done, boldly and defiantly done, by a free-soil court, our friends of the Republican party see no wrong in it, but applaud it, as a righteous act of judicial independence—a recognition of what Governor Seward says is Mr. Lincoln's law, higher than a mere Constitution. The slave who was rescued, was as much his owner's property, as anything else he owned. So said the Supreme Court of the United States years and years ago. The man who, by violence, tried to get that slave away from his master's control, was accessory, if not principal, in a well-defined crime. The judgment of the court which sentenced him, was as valid as that which hangs a mail-robber or a pirate, or confiscates a bale of smuggled goods, or affirms a patent right. But according to the Republican code of morality, the end justifies the means, where slavery is concerned. Had the rescue been attended with murder, if the victim were the owner or marshal, it would have been justifiable in their eyes, and thus, by the fanaticism which is instilled into the Northern mind, at least that part of it which has reasoned itself into concurrence with these anti-slavery principles, all law is overthrown, property is wrested from its owner, and a plain provision of the Constitution is defied. And this, say what you please, is Republicanism. Judge Spalding, of Ohio, said truly: "No man is recognized as a Republican here, who will, for a moment, sustain this miserable law." And the history of the Wisconsin case of revolutionary resistance forms just now the staple of Republican literature, for it was but last week that through the post-office I received (as I dare say thousands like me did) one of what are called the Tribune Tracts, containing Mr. Lincoln's speech at the Cooper Institute, in which the Fugitive Slave Act is alluded to only in disparagement, and Senator Doolittle's defence of the Wisconsin outrage.

How, after all this, any man in his senses can talk of Southern aggression, is a mystery. How any man, with the consciousness that there is a great, well-organized combination, ramified over every Northern State, East and West, having for its object to facilitate the escape of slaves, can talk of the balance of practical wrong being against us, passes my limited comprehension. Accumulate, if need be, all that the most extreme men of the South have ever said, or threatened, or demanded, and it bears no comparison with this great practical, substantial, and increasing wrong. Ask the most or the least declamatory railer against the South, who is now marshalling the forces of Mr. Lincoln, to tell you what he means by Southern aggression, and he won't know what to say short of offensive generalities. Be more precise with him, if you please, and ask him what, in the seventy years of the Union, or the seven years of the war, or the ninety years of colonial relation, what wrong South Carolina ever did to Pennsylvania? The South has never stolen any of our property from us. It generally befriends us. When the North or the Northwest tries to take away our poor little Mint or Naval Asylum, Southern men vote with us. In former days, Southern men, Cheves, and Lowndes, and Calhoun, and McDuffie, and Preston (all Carolinians), defended us and our interests. The earliest recollections of my life are of the praises of William Lowndes, of South Carolina, the most conservative, and temperate, and philosophical of statesmen, who uttered that memorable precept, well worthy to be repeated, "that the Presidency was a post too high to be sought or to be refused;" and of William Drayton, also of South Carolina, who lived the end of his honoured life among us, and who, moderate Union man as he was, once said in the House of Representatives, that if it ever were seriously discussed whether the master has a right of property in his slave, no members could remain who represented the people of the States in which these are possessed. Passing beyond mere local considerations, I ask the men of peaceful industry to remember that more than once Southern statesmen have saved us from war with one or the other of the great powers of Europe,—that the great Southern staple holds the world in tribute, and more than anything keeps the peace,—that assured peace is worth all the protection which legislative commercial restrictions promise; and remembering all this, and bearing in mind what Northern fanaticism is doing—a vexatious, irritating, agitating fanaticism—all the time; that Mr. Lincoln is shaking his fist at the South, and telling them that no man is fit to be free, or shall be permitted to be free, who owns slaves; that Mr. Seward is venting his personal disappointment in blasts of fierce defiance, and Mr. Sumner is denouncing the usurpations of the Supreme Court; I ask again, of the candid and fair-minded Northern man, what is meant by the wrongs the South has ever done to us. If it be said that the opposition of the South to a protective tariff, to internal improvements by the General Government, is a wrong to us, I have only to say, in reply, that the South has a right to its opinions on these questions of national economy, and does not enforce them by corruption, as Republican New England did in 1857, but by reason and by votes, by persuasion and conviction. As to internal improvements, and especially a railway to the Pacific, I would rather see it deferred till the intervening States shall attain a growth to make it for themselves, than to have it made now by that great Northwestern route, the adoption of which is to galvanize the insolvent corporations which concentre at Chicago, and to turn the commerce of the West exclusively into the lap of our commercial rival. Pennsylvania's true interests, if she only knew them, do not lie in that direction, but in the South and Southwest, from which Republicanism, and Lincolnism, and Abolitionism, if triumphant, will forever divide us.

What, then, in this crisis, when the North, the compact, fanatical North—for such in its anti-slavery organization it is from the northern boundary of this Commonwealth, eastward and westward—is thus advancing in its conscious and aggressive power, and the South suspicious—I do not like to say timorous, though the feeling may well be excused, with the danger before them and around them—but almost desperate; what, then, I ask, is the duty, what the interest, what should be the attitude of Pennsylvania—this great State, that has never yet cast her controlling vote in favour of Abolitionism, or anything tainted with Abolitionism, but always with national and Union men, and on the side of the Constitution? Her vote now, if she will be true to her history and her great traditions, can save the nation and the Union. If she vote with the Northern candidate, Pennsylvania becomes, as one of your resolutions the other night said, the fag-end, or in more dignified phrase, the rear-guard of the great Abolition party, and is separated forever—for it is a step that cannot be retraced—from her natural allies of the South and Southwest. Yes, fellow-citizens, her natural allies of the South and Southwest; for I undertake to say that it can be demonstrated, aside from our vast and controlling interest in the prosperity of the Union as it is, that the bulk of the manufactured products of which we are so justly proud, and about which we are so properly solicitous, finds its market in the South, and especially the Southwest, or south of a parallel running due west. The best trade for our railways is of course the local trade, and next to it is that which comes from the southward and westward. In the "North American," of last week, I find this statement, which, I doubt not, is true, quoted from a Western paper:—

"Even with the advantage of your manufactures, New York sells to the West more of the kind of goods, if not of the very goods manufactured in Philadelphia, than does Philadelphia itself. The whole teeming valley of the Mississippi is within the commercial grasp of Philadelphia, to take as much of its trade as it thinks fit, and yet how very little of it does

Philadelphia control. How few merchants are there in this valley, *north of St. Louis*, who buy their goods at Philadelphia, or who regard it as a place where there is any prospect of being able to dó any business.''

And all this, and more than this, is to be put in jeopardy for what? What substantial end is to be obtained—what material interest is to be promoted by casting the vote of Pennsylvania for Mr. Lincoln, and harnessing her to the car of New York, the Northeast, and West. To this question, put without offence, we have a right to have a candid and explicit answer—not declamation about Southern aggression and freedom in the territories, free homes for free men, and such claptrap, but a precise answer.

What Pennsylvania or Philadelphia material interest will be promoted by Mr. Lincoln's election?—a candidate thus "fathered and thus husbanded," I can understand perfectly well why rival commercial interests may be. New England and the Northwest are quite content with things as they are. The fishing bounties will have a new lease of life, to which I do not at all object, and which I only refer to now as showing the snug, direct protection, which our friends down East have had so long. That great job of New York, the Collins line of steamers, with its dark and bloody memories, its unexpiated sacrifices of human life—its Arctic and Pacific, and the hundreds of human beings engulphed and forgotten, and its stupendous subsidy, will be revived. Mr. O. B. Matteson will resume his influence in Congress, but what, I again ask, will Pennsylvania or Philadelphia gain?

Our friends will perhaps reply, a tariff,—a protective tariff,—such a stringent tariff as my excellent friend Mr. Carey desires; or a specific duty on Pennsylvania iron, and a little care for Pennsylvania coal. Now without in any way questioning or admitting the necessity or the expediency of a change in the tariff, I may be permitted to express some doubt as to the certainty of any change for the better under Mr. Lincoln's rule, and to hint the clear conviction, that so far as a change in the character of the duties affecting our interests is concerned, Pennsylvania making, by her vote, a Kentucky statesman President, will have a better chance than if she surrenders to Lincoln and Sewardism. I have watched the game—the progress of the contest with great attention, and in all the array of States, which are claimed for Mr. Lincoln, not one hearty word, not a word of any kind, is ever said in favour of a tariff, except in Pennsylvania, or, to limit it more precisely, in one part of Pennsylvania (for my impression is that in all that part of our State, north and west, which in 1856 gave heavy votes to Mr. Fremont, there is an ominous silence about a tariff). The New York Republican Hand-Book, though edited by a Pennsylvanian translated to New York, while full of poisonous nonsense about slavery, has no word for a tariff. Perhaps the Republicans of New Jersey are in favour of a new tariff, but New England and New York, and the Northwest, are cold, and indifferent, and silent.

No one who bestows attention to this topic can avoid being struck by the persistent indifference, if not hostility, to Pennsylvania interests. A remarkable illustration of it occurred last week. Mr. Charles F. Adams, Chairman of the Committee of Manufactures in the Republican House of Representatives was brought here to address our citizens without distinction of party. He was expected to discuss questions relating to Pennsylvania, and in order to clinch this a great protectionist leader and controversialist (Mr. Carey) presided, and introduced him. For hours did Mr. Adams discourse in the temper, I am glad to say, of a scholar and a gentleman, stringing as has been well said, brilliant rhetoric on the black thread of anti-slavery, and attributing all evil and abuse to the predominance of what it is the fashion to call the slave power. BUT NOT ONE SINGLE WORD—LITERALLY

NOT ONE AS TO A TARIFF, OR PROTECTION,—OR SPECIFIC DUTIES, OR PENNSYLVANIA INTERESTS,—and the next day when the speech was reported, the leading organ of the tariff party here could not conceal its chagrin, saying, both in sorrow and in anger, that it was expected Mr. Adams would have said a great deal about protection, but that he had touched it very gently! Very gently indeed. Mr. Adams did not ruffle the most acute sensibility of the most extreme free trader. He was true to Massachusetts and the "New York Evening Post," and he was honestly silent, for he could not conscientiously say a word of encouragement to Pennsylvania.

Nay, further, when a few days ago the Republican Convention met at Syracuse, to nominate a governor and electoral ticket, the name of William C. Bryant, the free-soil, free-trade editor and poet, he, who so resolutely refused to discuss a tariff with Mr. Carey, was received as an elector at large, with vociferous and enthusiastic cheering, and the resolutions adopted began with one of ominous significance, considering the cold comfort given at Chicago to the Pennsylvania protectionists. You all remember the doubtful phrase, which the "Evening Post" said did not mean a tariff at all, which was adopted at Chicago. Out of sixteen propositions constituting what was there determined to be the Republican platform, ten have direct reference to slavery, one to the homestead law, which is thought to have a kindred relation, one to internal improvements, one (known as the Dutch plank) to naturalization, one to a Pacific Railroad, which of course means the Platte River route, in which Pennsylvania has no interest and our rival States a great deal, and the following ambiguous, oracular one, as to protection, which was all poor Pennsylvania, though she had nominated Mr. Lincoln and defeated Mr. Seward, could obtain:—

"12th. That while providing revenue for the support of the National Government by duties upon imports [imposts?], sound policy requires such an adjustment of these imposts, as to encourage the development of the industrial interests of the whole country, and we commend [the word is a very gentle one] that policy of national exchanges (?) which secures to the working-man liberal wages, to agriculture remunerating prices, to manufacturers and mechanics an adequate reward for their skill, labour, and enterprise, and to the nation commercial prosperity and independence."

Now I aver, taking into view that the idea of protection to domestic industry is a clear and precise one, requiring few words and plain words, it never before was so enveloped in obscure generalities; and, so apparent was this—so palpably inadequate was this wordy rhetoric to the just demands of our Pennsylvania protectionists—that, when the Lincoln ratification meeting was held in this city, if my memory serves me, it was deemed absolutely necessary to invigorate this emasculation of tariff doctrine; to put a gloss on it, which would make it suit Schuylkill and Centre and Alleghany counties; and accordingly, Mr. Henry C. Carey, the champion of protection, a gentleman to whose patriotic and conscientious convictions on this topic, I do willing justice, offered an amended series of resolutions, to put this matter right. This, if I mistake not, was about the time he was defying Mr. Bryant,—the craven knight of free trade,—to mortal conflict in the newspapers. This being the state of the record, the great New York Convention meets, as I have said, at Syracuse, with enthusiasm, puts this same Mr. Bryant at the head of the Lincoln electoral ticket, and coolly and contemptuously tells the Pennsylvania protectionists, that they shall have no influence, and must let the Chicago platform alone, and take it with all its obscurities. The Report reads thus:—

"Hon. Benjamin Welsh, Jr., announced with pleasure, that the Committee on Resolutions had found no difficulty in agreeing, and had directed him unanimously to report the following:

"Resolved, That this Convention, representing the Republican electors of the State of

New York, heartily accepts and adopts the Resolutions of the National Republican Convention held at Chicago, and that it has no disposition *to alter one line or word* of that masterly and patriotic declaration of principles."

Who but Pennsylvania had asked to alter a line or word, and what does this mean but what I have already hinted at, that the Lincoln communities; the whole array, which I can but describe as the free railroad iron States, New England, and New York, and Illinois, and Michigan, and Wisconsin, and Iowa, and Minnesota, and the New York counties of Pennsylvania, through which is now secretly running a foreign railroad, to steal the Ohio trade from us, means to use this great commonwealth as a beast of burden, harnessed to the abolition, free-trade wagon of Abraham Lincoln and Hannibal Hamlin, and then to cheat her afterwards. Depend on it, if Pennsylvania, vigilant of her interests, has to choose between two schools of free trade, that which is candidly and manfully and honestly professed by the South, and that which is in masquerade in the North and East, her chance will be better with the first, for all the tariff she needs (especially if she earns confidence and gratitude by fidelity to the Constitution, the Union, and the adjudicated rights of the South), than if led away from the path in which she has always walked; turned from the safe Democratic groove in which she has always moved; she trusts herself to that vast conglomeration of fanatical and mercenary communities, and bankrupt railroad corporations—for such, almost without exception, are the Northern and Northwestern railroad companies—which at this moment constitute the great Lincoln army of the North.

And now comes the question, what shall she do? What shall the honest yeomanry of Pennsylvania—what shall the business men of this great commonwealth do in October and November next? Shall they vote for the anti-slavery candidate,—for such, without offence or dispute, Mr. Lincoln may be said to be,—or for John C. Breckinridge, whom his enemies describe, and we are content to take, as the Southern or Southwestern candidate; for Andrew G. Curtin, Mr. Lincoln's deputy, of Centre County, or Henry D. Foster, a modest, able, patriotic man, against whom, to this time, no whisper of reproach has been levelled?

John C. Breckinridge—waiving for the present all objection, arising out of the pending canvass, which shall be hereafter fairly considered—stands before the people of this country as a man with singular qualities of personal popularity, especially in Pennsylvania and New Jersey.

There is, between them and Kentucky, a close sympathy, which, if it be but a sentiment, is one that has always existed. Henry Clay, and James Guthrie, and John C. Breckinridge, have always had their most earnest friends here. It would seem as if there was a congeniality of temper. There is something, too, in historical and geographical relations. The great river which washes the borders and receives the tributaries of Kentucky, virtually has its source in Pennsylvania. From Western Pennsylvania, the farmer, the manufacturer, even the lumberman, as he goes with his products to market, is at home in Kentucky, and its trade is almost a local trade for us. Judging from commercial results, Kentucky seems to cling more closely and affectionately to Pennsylvania, than she does to her own mother Virginia; and what man in Pennsylvania looks with alien eye on Kentucky, even though she be a Southern and slave-owning State? Mr. Breckenridge's familiar relations are interwoven with us and with New Jersey. The names of those to whom he owes his being, of John Witherspoon and Samuel Stanhope Smith, and whose great example he has never dishonoured, are household words in our sister State, and adorn especially her great institution of learning, of which she is justly proud, and which sometimes seems to belong in a measure to us,—so many Pennsylvanians having there been nurtured,—where were educated Madison, and Sergeant, and Gaston, and Dallas, and Frelinghuysen, and Ingersoll.

These are what, of themselves, would make the Democratic candidate popular in the Middle States, but—individualizing the subject more closely—let any man study the career of Mr. Breckinridge himself, yet a young man, and the secret of his popularity is plainly revealed. Until called by the popular voice to the second office of the nation, his career was that of the legislator merely, so far as political duties are involved, and it was distinguished, from first to last, by the high-spirited, high-toned bearing, which, in a parliamentary body more than anywhere, makes its mark. There was no reserve in his opinions—no equivocation in his course. All was manly and straightforward, and patriotic. During the Mexican war, when a call was made for volunteers, John C. Breckinridge was among those who answered that appeal. He followed the flag of his country in its march of triumph, and when the war was over, returned to the pursuits of civil life, without restlessness or repining.

And this is the man—this is the Kentucky statesman—he who for four years past has been the presiding officer of the great representative body of the sovereign States of the Union, of that body which especially represents the equality of the States; this is the man whom it suits an unscrupulous partisan press to denounce as a sectionalist and a disunionist. I regret to be made to believe that this unjust accusation comes from a fragment of the Democratic party—not, I hope, from Judge Douglas, but from Judge Douglas's emissaries and organs. It may, from motives of policy, find a faint echo from the friends of Mr. Bell; but they know it is unjust. Republicans do not venture to hint it. Mr. Adams, the other night, expressly disavowed it. Now I ask, in all candour, what, in Mr. Breckinridge's antecedents, remote or immediate, is there to countenance such a suspicion? Has he ever said a word, or done a deed, that looks like it? If he has, I ask for its production. Surely, his thinking that Congress cannot prohibit slavery in a territory, does not make him sectional. Judge Douglas and his school proclaim this, and Mr. Bell and Mr. Crittenden agree to it. Believing the Missouri Compromise line to be unconstitutional or unwise, does not imply sectionalism; for so thought John M. Clayton, a Whig Secretary of State, and it was a Whig Senator from Kentucky who moved its repeal. To hold that, until a State government is organized, slavery, and all kindred subjects are beyond the interference of local legislation, is no crime, for the Supreme Court has so decided it; and it is only the wild radical or fanatic who does not recognize its authority. What, then, is it that gives colour to this, the only and the desperate charge made against Mr. Breckinridge? It is that the delegates who nominated him were from the Southern States mainly (not alone, for Pennsylvania then, as now, was with him), and that, in the calculation of chances, Southern electoral votes are counted on to elect him.

It is no fault of Mr. Breckinridge or his friends that it is so. It would suit the Abolition leaders in the North very well indeed, to see a divided and distracted South, if they could manage, by the substantial agency of Mr. Douglas, or the mythical influence of another party, to divide the compact array of those States, whose property and very existence are threatened from without. I do not believe they can—but if they do—if the South is not true now to its friends in the North, it must depend on itself hereafter. If this could be accomplished, all would be well, and there would be no need of further defamation or disparagement. But when the South, baited and besieged, retires within itself, proclaims its defensive principles, and then, instead of taking one of its own men—I mean taking a man from what is called the extreme South—advances to the Northern frontier, and selects as its Presidential candidate a Kentucky statesman (Kentucky being in point of fact a Middle State), is it not the rankest injustice to say, that a candidate so chosen and so sustained, is sectional? I wonder at the shameless effrontery which can say it, or the stupid credulity which adopts it. It is conceded that Mr. Breckinridge cannot be elected without the vote of Pennsylvania or New York and New Jersey, and it is as clear an assumption, that neither State can be carried for any man who threatens or doubts the stability of the Union. I, and thousands like me, claiming to act with and under the Democratic organization of the Middle States, support and ask you to support Mr. Breckinridge, because we *know* him to be national, and believing he will carry every Southern and Southwestern State, we think every social, political, and material interest that Pennsylvania has at stake, will be incalculably promoted by his success.

One thing more and I have done, for I am quite aware I have trespassed too much on you, but I desire to do an act of justice. I have heard another objection to Mr. Breckinridge. It is in the mouths of factious and disappointed men, and in the torrent of bitter injustice which is foaming around us it is sometimes assumed to be true, and its justice is conceded by those who should know better. It is said Mr. Breckinridge is the administration—the President's candidate, and as it is the fashion always to defame and abuse an outgoing administration—a President whose patronage is exhausted, this of course is thought a grievous stigma. In the first place the fact is not so. He is no more the candidate of this administration than he was of the last—no more Mr. Buchanan's than General Pierce's. Before the nomination, or the Convention at Charleston and Baltimore, neither the President, nor any member of his cabinet, that I am aware of, ever uttered one word in favour of Mr. Breckinridge. Nor did his office-holders, who are supposed, whether rightly or wrongly I don't care to inquire, to take their colour from the tree on which they feed. I incline very much to think they were the other way. This I well know, that there never was a more fatal mistake committed than by the Reading Convention in failing to nominate (as it could have done), and to instruct our delegates to support as a unit Mr. Breckinridge. Had this been done, as some of us desired, there would have been no division in the Democratic ranks, and John C. Breckinridge would have been the nominee of a united and triumphant party. Why it was not done, I do not care to inquire.

When, however, the action of the Convention was determined, and the two candidates, Mr. Breckinridge and Mr. Douglas, were placed before the nation, the President—like any other citizen—the President's friends, like all others in or out of office, had a right to make a choice, and to express a preference. They have done so, and they do so now, and they rest that preference on a principle. They predicate of Mr. Breckinridge's administration a faithful adherence to a great constitutional principle of equality of rights to citizens of all the States in the common territories, to be divested neither by Congress nor the creation of a Congress—a territorial legislature—and so thinking, they sustain him. To this extent only is Mr. Breckinridge connected with or supported by the President.

But I do not choose—it would be rank injustice if I did—to put this on so narrow a ground. The confidence and support of a statesman so well-trained, of so large experience, and thorough familiarity with the working of the great machine of our constitutional system, are not to be disclaimed; and Mr. Breckinridge may well be proud of possessing them. No one better knows the executive responsibility, and the tax on physical and intellectual energy which the chief magistracy of the country imposes. No one can have been at Washington, and had a chance of watching the load of care and labour resting on one man, and how it is borne, without feeling the gross injustice of the disparagement of which the President has been and is the object. I have had some opportunities of observation, having been to a certain extent connected with the Government; and I should think myself faithless to every obligation of gratitude and justice, if I did not bear my testimony, be it worth much or little, in his support. He has been my friend; and if any one present or absent thinks what I say of no value, merely because I have received honours and confidence at Mr. Buchanan's hands, I am very sure that no one will think the worse of me as a gentleman and man of honour for choosing to be grateful. Let me refer for an instant to what has been done in our foreign policy, which accidentally has most attracted my attention, and seems to be entirely lost sight of by the scavengers who are engaged in raking up in all the alleys and byways materials of defamation. So busy are we in devouring with morbid greediness Covode reports, and such wretched trash, that we hardly pause to reflect that, through his temperate and most circumspect policy, Mr. Buchanan has given to this country four years of absolute and assured peace with foreign nations. Among the prejudices invoked to defeat his election in 1856 was the Ostend manifesto, which, his enemies said, pledged him to a restless and aggressive policy all over the world.

When General Cass was chosen Secretary of State, a war or some sort of difficulty with Great Britain was foretold as certain. Instead of which, there has been absolute repose. Each of the three preceding administrations had its irritations: Mr. Clayton quarrelled with a French Minister; Mr. Marcy dismissed an English one; Mr. Webster had sharp controversy with Austria; and Mr. Everett had somthing like a squabble with a Central American one. Since Mr. Cass has had charge of the Department there has been trouble nowhere. Surely, for this some credit is due to the President and his administration. Be it remembered, too, that, at the beginning, the state of things, especially between the United States and Great Britain, could not be said to be propitious. That parent of perplexity, the Clayton-Bulwer Treaty—the compact by which two clever men thought each had overreached the other, and which no two men, representing each party, have been able to construe alike since—was in the path; Central America was more perplexed than ever. A new treaty with reference to it had been made in London, which the President did not approve, but which, in justice to the negotiators, and especially to Great Britain, which might have misunderstood his action, he submitted to the Senate. The Senate amended, and the British Ministry rejected it, and it lay in its obstructive fragments on top of the Clayton-Bulwer bargain. This was still unpropitious. The courteous and friendly temper of the President, aided perhaps by a change of Ministry in England, was keeping the atmosphere tranquil, when the public was startled by the news that the English cruisers had renewed in a most offensive form the belligerent right of search. It was an anxious moment. It was, I think, in the recess of Congress. The President sent all the available naval force into the West India seas, with orders to resist. The danger, thanks to the good sense prevalent all round, passed away. Again, Great Britain and France solicited the Government to unite in their quasi war with China. Mr. Buchanan refused; and, without dwelling on it here, I need only remind you of the rich reward we have had, in continuing peace in the East as well as the West. When the San Juan affair occurred, what could have been more considerate and statesmanlike than the conduct of the President? He thought the military officer wrong, and disavowed him, with as little hesitancy as when, with different objects, he had sent the navy to the Gulf, when he knew we were right. The employment of General Scott was an act which commanded approval everywhere. In all things Mr. Buchanan's foreign policy has been that of peace and conciliation. He has repressed filibusterism with a strong hand. He has done more to suppress the foreign slave-trade than all who have gone before him; and if his negotiations with Mexico and Spain have failed, it has been through no fault of his. Had the Republican minority in the Senate consented to the Mexican Treaty, we should at least have had a better chance of pacification in that afflicted nation than now, when Old Spain seems to be clutching at her colonies again, and everything in our close neighbourhood is confusion and bloodshed. The Spanish Treaty was rejected under a false pretext, that it absolutely recognized a claim for the Amistad negroes, when in fact there was no such recognition, but a reference of it, with other questions, to a tribunal for adjudication. It was the President's treaty, and therefore it was rejected. Throughout, Mr. Buchanan's policy—and to this I challenge contradiction—has been that of dignity, of judicions energy and peace.

I am quite aware that I expose myself to a sneer, in passing by, as I am compelled to do, his domestic policy. When I left America, in the summer of 1857, the Kansas excitement was in full fury, and a civil war, as seemed to be conceded on all sides, imminent. I returned after an absence of less than two years, and I found that excitement existing merely on the page of history, and kept in recollection only to gratify party animosity. The fall of the year which witnessed Mr. Buchanan's inauguration was memorable from a great financial and commercial crisis, for which he certainly was not responsible. In that crisis the credit of the Government stood firm. There are those who can remember other and less severe commercial convulsions, when the credit of the Government fell with private credit. As lately as 1841, the public loans, which never for a moment within three years have been damaged, were spurned by every great and every petty banking-house in Europe. And now, these four years of alleged misrule over—now, when the scars of private distress and shattered individual credit, though fresh, are healing, no honest man who looks over the wide expanse of our country, its universal contentment, its recuperating energies, which are sufficient to neutralize the false economy of States and the ruinous working of a system of inflated credit, will venture to say that all this is in spite of misgovernment, or be unwilling, unless blinded by excess of party animosity, to give some share of praise to the Chief Magistrate, the closing days of whose trust are thus prosperous. So much I have felt bound to say. The time is not distant when, all the irritations of the hour past, history will do its work of justice.

I have detained you too long. Mine are the first words from Pennsylvania lips that have been spoken for John C. Breckinridge. They have not been inconsiderately uttered. They are probably my last; for I must leave to others the active conduct of this campaign, willing to be a private soldier in the ranks. I shall have my full reward, if what I have uttered to-night shall not be in vain. They are meant to embody the latent and real feeling of this community—to inspire energy—to repress discord—to conciliate—to give form and substance to that national sentiment which nowhere has more force than in Pennsylvania. What I have said has been earnestly said. I hope it has given pain to no one.

APPENDIX.

The case of rescue of a prisoner convicted by the United States authorities, is that of Booth, reported in 21 Howard. The "National Intelligencer," of to-day contains the following intelligence, extracted from a Wisconsin paper:—

"The Milwaukee 'News of the West,' of the 29th ultimo, gives an account of the second attempt of the United States Marshal to arrest Sherman M. Booth, who recently escaped from confinement inflicted for aiding in the rescue of a fugitive slave. Mr. McCarty, the United States Marshal, with six men, went to the house of Mr. Pickett, where he supposed Booth had been secreted. Pickett's house was surrounded by the officers, and Pickett, as soon as he saw the officer, attempted to strike him. Mr. McCarty then asked him if Booth was secreted in his house, and informed him that he had a warrant for his arrest. Pickett replied that he had been there, but had gone away. At this time Pickett shouted 'Help, for God's sake!' when a terrible commotion began to be heard in the house, and thirteen other men, armed with guns, pistols, and pitchforks, came from the interior of the dwelling, and surrounded the officers, threatening their lives if they did not leave the premises. These demonstrations aroused the suspicions of the officers, who now began to doubt the truth of Pickett's assertion, that Booth had left the house.

"They were proceeding to search the house, when Pickett desired that he might be permitted to put on some more clothing; and, upon being released, seized a horn hanging near, and gave one blast upon it. It was immediately taken from him, but was answered in a dozen different directions, and men were seen coming from all quarters, armed with guns and pitchforks. They immediately added themselves to the force already collected, and commenced threatening the lives of the officers, and aiming their guns at their breasts. Very soon after, armed men began to arrive in wagons; and, in the short space of one hour and a half, sixty-two men had gathered together, thus outnumbering the officers nearly twelve to one. Some twenty-five men ranged themselves in order, and, pointing their guns at McCarty and his men, ordered them to leave. One of them had his gun cocked, and became so much excited that he discharged it, the ball entering a barn near.

"The mob then demanded of McCarty what he intended to do? He boldly and emphatically replied, that 'he came there to take Booth, and that if he could get sight of him, he should accomplish his purpose, or die in the attempt. That the men who were with him were determined men, and if violence was offered, it must be done at their peril.' Mr. McCarty then asked them their purpose. They replied that Booth should never be taken, except over their bodies; *that they defied the Government*, and that no power on earth could get him from them. Again they demanded that the Marshal should depart, but he coolly informed them that he was not yet ready, and asked their names. A large number immediately stepped up and gave them, together with their places of residence, coupled with the assertions *that they would 'lynch, shoot, and quarter' every Government officer who attempted to accomplish Booth's arrest.*

"McCarty did not deem it advisable to risk the lives of six, against twelve times that number, and, not knowing that Booth was in the house, did not desire to peril their lives against such fearful odds, or render himself liable if the fugitive was not there secreted. He sent to Ripon for reinforcements, but informed the crowd that if Booth was seen or they would admit his whereabouts, he would take him or perish. He waited until eleven o'clock, having been there in the face of loaded rifles and desperate men, some seven hours, when, assistance not arriving, himself and men quietly departed."

PHILADELPHIA, September 4th.

www.ingramcontent.com/pod-product-compliance
Lightning Source LLC
LaVergne TN
LVHW020636110826
845149LV00004B/1222